Poems from the Arrowhead Clubhouse

Poems from the Arrowhead Clubhouse

Arrowhead Clubhouse

To order additional copies of this book, contact:
Xlibris
844-714-8691
www.Xlibris.com
Orders@Xlibris.com
808589

Arrowhead Clubhouse Mission Statement

*Arrowhead's mission is to support our members who suffer from
a serious chronic mental illness on their journey to recovery.
This is done by creating opportunities through the use of our
facility, support programs, our housing initiative, and
our ability to build a bridge with a wider community.*

Arrowhead Community Creative Writing Workshop

In 2017, a group of individuals gathered every other Friday at the Arrowhead Clubhouse to explore Creative Writing ideas, styles and thoughts around a theme. We wrote togeth- er, but also on our own.

The patina of our creativity, humour, and honesty shades the pages where we laid down the power of our words for our own viewing, which we now share with you in this publica- tion.

Core contributors were Marie, Suzanne, Melanie, & Brian. Additional contributors included Pam, Justine, Sheena, Lisa, Faux, Kristops, & Janet.

The members would like to thank the wonderful Jeanne Sommerfield who facilitated the creative writing workshops and the marvelous Jane Covernton who helped us create this beautiful publication.

Rain/Hard Day's Night

It's been such a long winter…
Depressed. Gloomy. Shut in.
Rain. Rain. Rain.
Get naked at home.
Jump in the shower-warm up!
Wrap up in a blue silk robe. Jump in bed.
Read a book, Charles Dickens 'Bleak House'.
Rain on the roof… pitter patter like Thomas the cat.
Loud like thunder. Fearful noise.
Safe. Comfortable. At home.

By Marie, Suzanne, Christie, Brian, Pam, Justine, Janet

Food Bank Egg

Don't sit there! Why?
There's an egg!
Who laid that egg?
A food bank egg
From a Rhode Island Red
Fresh from the Creek.
The chicken was fresh, not so the egg.
The egg is on the chair.
The egg is everywhere.
On the floor there is more.
Broken egg. Rejected egg. Donated egg.
Here it is. All cracked up.
Brian has the plan to clean it off the floor.
Mop & bucket—mess no more!
The evidence is on the chair. Everywhere.
Broken.

By Marie, Suzanne, Brian, Christie, Sheena

Wind - This We Know

Breezy, stormy, cool, warm, gusty.
Quiet, deafening, peaceful, exhilarating.
Soft, stinging, pushing, pulling.

Sometimes there's no wind - less air - hard to breathe.
Capture with sails, flags, clothes on the line,
Birds on the wing, clouds flow slowly by.
Blowing soft as a kitten, harsh as an insult.
Warm as a teddy bear, or a favourite blanket.

Cold as being lonely.
Ocean spray from sculpted waves.
Swirling snowflakes from winter's blast.

We are buffeted by life's winds.
How do we survive the force?
Our souls stand strong.
Sturdy as an old oak tree,
With roots deep in our community.

By Pam & Marie

My Teddy Bear

Allie is…
Soft & cuddly, comforting, fuzzy,
Held with love in my arms.
A Prairie bear from Saskatchewan.
A remembering gift, a happy gift.
She is always with me!

By Pam

Between Myself & I

I keep it in my head
Between myself & I.
Sadness, anxiety, questions.
Answers? Maybe not. Pieces.
A puzzle in my head.
Things I'm afraid to say out loud.
Anger- not being good enough.
Black. 'In the End' by Linkin Park.
Wallow for awhile. Too Negative.
A part of you that says "Move On!"
History. Settling the future.
That's how it is. Me. Stuff.
Some comfort…

By Marie, Suzy, Lisa, Melanie

Self Esteem Gives You Freedom

A reflection.
Positive feeling about yourself.

I don't like the mirror.
Moving forward. Find the Positive.

Self esteem increasing with age
And accomplishments.

Like yourself. Like your morals. Strength.
Knowing. Accountable to myself.

Action.
Throw away the Negative.

Positive thoughts that create motion.
Share a part of Yourself.

Pride. Content. Self-assured. Reliable.
Consistent as the ocean.

Allowing the waves of emotion to flow naturally.
Without drowning.
Freedom.

By Marie, Lisa, Suzy, Melanie

I Want YOU to See ME

The good:
Personality
Reluctant matriarch
Humour
Charisma
Creativity
Survival
Beauty within
Smile
Faith
Rising out of the ashes
Hazel eyes, brown eyes
Humanity
Health
Compassion
Love
Kindness niceness
Loyalty
Wellness
Steadfastness
Different coloured hair
Bleeding hearts
Warmth
Resilience

By Marie, Suzy, Melanie, Lisa

In our garden

In our garden there would be weeds.
Or it might be a rock garden…
Planted with seeds,
sand and rock in a different pattern.
Rings 'round stones like rings 'round Saturn.

Big leaves, small leaves, mostly green.
A different mood for every scene.
Flowers around me, I feel the peace.
My distractions for a moment cease.
Nature and man working side by side.
Admiring life and taking pride.

Behind the hedge, I hear a sound…
Rippling, lulling all around.
Beyond my stillness I want to see;
The cool water is
inviting me.

In my mind,
I make this place
To visit when
I need some
space…

By Marie & Melanie

I wouldn't sell…

Me. I am not for sale.
However, I feely give my …
Advice. (No charge!)
Love. Unconditional.
Gratitude. Not often enough…
Comfort.
Hugs. Not just because it's expected.
Friendship. Deeper than 'acquaintance'.
Food. To those in need.
Time. Give back to the universe the gifts I have to offer.

By Marie, Melanie, Suzy.

Conscience, Go Away

My conscience talks to me:
'I should have, I shouldn't have'.
The language of 'should' makes me question.
Makes me aware.
Makes me think.
Makes me care.
Makes me worry - the Golden Rule -
Did I make someone look the fool?
Is it fluid? Does it change?
All thoughts get rearranged.
Another point of view. I have my own,
But so do you.
Conscience gives us balance,
But may follow another path…
Spiralling. Feeding on itself. Landing in guilt.
It could be the Dark Side.
It can polarize our thoughts, and take us on a ride.
It may be taught, it may be learned.
Do I care? Am I concerned?

By Marie, Suzy, Brian, Sheena, Faux

The Mystifying Mist

A terrifying, hiding, mystifying mist,
unknown shores protected by rocky reefs.
Listen for breaking waves,
watery markers of unseen dangers.
Perception offers untrustworthy sensory information.
The Spanish galleon becalmed within a
blanket of delusion,
the creaking rigging and flapping sail
hide the sound of a breaking whale.

By Brian

Change

No bother to some,
A chance to look forward to something new.
Depending on the path of change...
Hateful to some.
New schedules...day to day stuff.
Order.
But I like order too!
My house in order.
My clock in order,
Change with the change.
Walk from old to new.
No room in my life for the new fridge relationships!
Throw it out? Sometimes you have to.
I'm not attached to my stuff -- just people and pets.
Change can break things.
Change can make things...
Better.
Moving in with Mom is a good change.
When someone dies, it's not. It hurts.
Change within my control is good.
Willpower. On the path to happiness.
Physical change -- pain -- not one good thing about it!
...forced upon me by this falling-apart body.

by Marie and Suzy

Mirror

The mirror is reflective,
It can make life seem magic.
This process is selective,
It also shows the tragic.

Woman's beauty neglected,
A sorrow to the masses,
But it keeps her protected,
From the vulgar man's passes.

A product for vanity,
For making things clearer,
It can affect sanity,
If you believe the mirror.

By Melanie Elizabeth

GOSSIP

Ring-a-ling Ting-a-ling
Sing a thing Bing
Phone drone moan tone
Groan in an alone bone.

Chitter bitter sitter
Quitter litter fritter
Ba-boom-boom
Assume or resume

Clatter and shatter with flatter
Matter to platter makes fatter.
Mean bean the Queen
Seen causing a scene pristine.

By Melanie Elizabeth

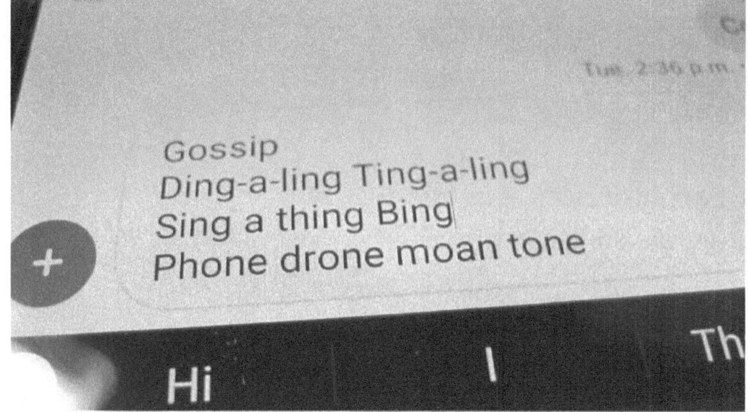

Who's In Charge?

Might is Right. The Monsters.
Warfare. Genocide. Human Trafficking.
Panoramic Pandemic.
Fear. People are afraid - Depressed - Despairing.
Cold blue fear.
Shut-down fear.
False evidence appearing Real.

Courage is needed. Decide to survive.
Nature is Nurture. Self Empowerment.
Non-alignment creates Diversity. Creativity.
I am in charge.
Emotions. Thinking. Choices. Response.
Mindfulness.

When evil becomes too much,
overwhelming your being,
preventing your eyes from really seeing
the horrors around you taking place,
fear is haunting every face.
I reflect inwards to inner space
to change the focus from within
to reflect the joy found in that place.

By Brian, Kristops, Marie

The Ride

He's ushered in with alot of care
Hoping that everyone he will spare.
Clawing, jumping - eyes of steel,
Am I going ride him - is this real?
Carefully lowering onto his back
Don't let the rope give any slack.
I say a silent prayer for me
To actually another day to see.
They open the chute and let him loose
Riding like sitting on a bull moose.
Bucking, tossing me from side to side
Please, I need this seven second ride.
My spurs don't dent his mighty skin
I suddenly feel sick deep within.
Through the air I seem to soar,
Slamming down on the arena floor.
He's coming at me while I am down
Where oh where is that rodeo clown?
Full speed ahead I run like Hell
To safety where the story I can tell
How I managed to run away
And escape the bull who can also say
Another one on my list of casualties
I really wonder if they have all their faculties...

By Marie

The Attack

Bombs go off, you hear a scream
They think that it's all a dream
Children running, bodies falling
Parents waiting, they are calling
Give my child a chance to live
A life where they can always give

Blood is pooling by the door
Several bodies on the floor
Police, ambulance to the call
They try hard to save them all.
But for some, it is too late
Succumbing to their awful fate

Attackers, they all are sinners
Thinking they are the winners

But do you know what they did wrong?
United us and made us strong

By Marie

The Gum Incidents

The gum stuck to the sole of my shoe.
Why is it that gum jumps and lands exactly where I'm about
to place my foot? Then it comes to me: you remember in
all those old comics and movies, detectives were known as
"gum-shoes?"

Now, we all know there are all kinds of crimes punishable
by law. But just suppose that me, with gum on my shoe, has
now become an official amateur "gum-shoe." Now, I'll try
and find things that should be crimes.

Trying to look inconspicuous, I saunter along on the look- out for
future law-breakers. Then, walking west, I see an elderly gentleman
advancing toward me on his motorized scooter. Of course, he is
smack-dab in the middle of the sidewalk. Does he move over a
few inches so we can both use the sidewalk? The answer is "no."
I have to step off the curb onto the street. Future crime number
one - uncovered!

Feeling quite satisfied with myself, I continue. Then, I spot it!
Someone is actually allowing their beloved canine to pee on the tire
of a parked car. They don't try to stop him. After all, poochie is on
a leash and you can't really clean "that" up. Future crime number
two - uncovered!

I'm getting a bit tired now, so I think I'll just try to spot one more. I
am just passing a local bus shelter where, sitting quite comfortably,

are three big, strapping young men. At this moment, an elderly lady, pushing a cart, approaches. She is obviously waiting for the bus.

But did even one of these young men offer his seat? Of course not! So there she stood and there they sat. Unbeliev- able! Future crime number three - uncovered.

I can feel it now. The glob of gum is wearing off my shoe.
I guess my time as an amateur "gum-shoe" has ended. But
just as a reminder, the next time a piece of gum sticks on the
bottom of your shoe - think of the fun you can have.

By Marie

The Inferno

A lightning strike or just a spark
Ignites the inferno - all is dark.
Grass and trees, they feel the blaze
As it travels in its craze.
Panic's there - will all be lost?
Homes and animals are the cost
Of spreading, fiery blast.
Who knows how long it will last.
The winds blow strong to fuel the flames
Do we know who is to blame?
Mother Nature or simple folk
Who toss away their precious smoke.
For these people who lost it all
Reach out to them - give them a call
To help them in their time of woe
And pray that time soon will show
They still have heart and will to live
Rebuild again, their strength will give
Them hopes and dreams to start again
Praying this terror soon will end.

By Marie

The Weather and Me

The blazing sun scorches the ground.
Not a cloud to be seen around.
Even though the breezes blow
There's no relief that it does show
My skin is hot - on fire it seems
Glowin g red from the sun's bright beams.
It's hard to breathe; there is no air
My energy's gone - it isn't fair
That I can feel the inner heat
With every time my heart does beat.
It makes me angry, my patience worn

Know Me

Know me now, just as you can
Maybe you'll become my biggest fan.
A friend forever I will be
In good times, bad
times you will see.

Inner faith I have within
True and loyal I've
always been.
Patience, not a virtue,
I'm afraid
But love for others
will never fade

Anger does not
often show
But can be present if I know
Someone has harassed my friend
And I'll defend him to the end.

There is beauty in all I see
And I'm as happy as I can be
But I warn you now - don't cross the line
You may regret it - but guaranteed - I will be fine.

By Marie

My Perfect Canada

Canada-great land of the free,
If I were boss, this is how it would be.
No more hunger, pain or drugs,
Just love and laughter, smiles and hugs.
No matter the color of the race,
With each other, we shall embrace.

No more homeless there would be,
All have housing as you will see.
Pure, clean water and pure fresh air,
Is something that we all will share.
Can this be fantasy for me and you?
Not for me-it's my dream come true.

By Marie

www.ingramcontent.com/pod-product-compliance
Lightning Source LLC
Chambersburg PA
CBHW051424250726
48655CB00003B/1225